Spaghetti Brain

Reagan Motsinger

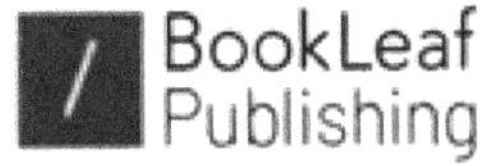

Presentation by *BookLeaf Publishing*

Web: www.bookleafpub.com

E-mail: info@bookleafpub.com

ISBN: 9789357611619

First edition 2022

ACKNOWLEDGEMENT

I owe many thanks to my mom for encouraging me to continue publishing poetry. I would also like to thank my poetry professor, Dr. Amy Ash, for helping expand my view of what poetry can be and for the assignments that produced several poems in this book. I also want to thank BookLeaf for the opportunity to publish my work again.

"when facing the feelings i've let consume me" was inspired by Luke Hemmings's *When Facing the Things We Turn Away From*. The poem uses lyrics and variations of lyrics from many songs on the album.
"reality blurred" was inspired by 5 Seconds of Summer's "Long Way Home."
"warrior" was inspired by a random writing prompt off Pinterest, so if whoever created that prompt ever sees this, shoutout to you. :)
"my grief" quotes the line "screaming, crying perfect storm" from Taylor Swift's "Blank Space."
"Celestine" enters the mind of one of the protagonists of the fantasy novel I hope to

publish in the near future (and that's all I'm going to say on the subject).

when facing the feelings i've let consume me

- inspired by Luke Hemmings's *When Facing the Things We Turn Away From*

lately i've been living in a whirlwind,
my life no longer feeling like my own. i slog
through my days without a moment to take

a breath, an endless string of work i can barely
bear and meetings i can barely find the energy
to care for. everything feels wrong, nothing feels

right. i run, but my feet are trapped in quicksand,
my motions don't even feel like my own. i am
an automaton, a scripted creature
so steeped in stress

that i can't feel anything in response to my burn-
out. it is just my state of being now.
it feels so long since i stood
at that starting line, filled with fresh

promise and possibility for the months
ahead. now i look back

with a cold tin heart, exhausted, angry,
and confused. where did the time go? i've been

so consumed with doing things that i missed out
on so many other opportunities. have i
wasted my time? what can i do with the rest
of it when the future is so uncertain?

betrayed, burnt out, overwhelmed, anxious.
everything hurts, so nothing does. numb,
i bob out to sea,
a lone message in a bottle with no connections
to tether it to any one shore.

i had this picture of what this phase of my life
would be like, but now i am not the same girl
who envisioned them. she was optimistic, and i
yearn to be her again, impossible as that

may be. i'm missing memories that were never
even mine; it wasn't real, and i can
never go back and play out that vision.
i can't change things, and i don't know
if i'm falling or drowning in this mess

that has become my life. drowning out the fires
only results in a flood; either way,
my eyes are open

to watch the horror unfold,
and the music crescendos
in one final song for my sanity.

i'm broken and scarred, but like a diamond, i
shine even still. it's all a performance i put on
to convince everyone i'm fine, a mirage
on repeat. little do they know
i'm dying inside, craving connection

and calm that i can't find here anymore.

ars poetica

Once upon a time, I believed my writing
was utterly separate from myself,
that I could write in a void unafflicted
by the troubles and pains of the world

around me. That couldn't be further
from the truth. Writing my stories
calms my emotions; it puts me in someone
else's head for a while, and the lingering
anger and sadness can subside, but that
doesn't mean they aren't spliced to my life.

Now I see where threads of reality weave
in with the fabric of fantasy and poetry,
the connections, inferences, ideas that peek
through the gaps. Maybe I'm not as subtle

as I thought. Oh, who am I kidding? I've never
been subtle. But perhaps I'm cleverer
than I ever imagined. I have miles
of inspirational thread around me
to pull from, so surely there is
something worth twisting into a tale.

look up to the stars

Swirling stars splattered
on a dark blanket of sky,
twisting and twirling into
marvelous shapes or simple
designs for humanity
to embellish with storytelling.

The moon glows bright
to illuminate the sky, and it seems
unfair that it doesn't cast its own
spotlight down on the world below.
Winking planets and passing
planes gaze down at us,
serene and silent as most
of the world sleeps. Not me, though.

I like to watch them in return
and soak in the whimsy that the stars
supply to this dark world.

trapped.

Have you ever wanted to scream,
but known that no matter how loud it gets
or how long the sound lasts, no amount of noise
can purge the pain from your soul?

Have you ever had so much anger bubble up
inside you that when you try to finally
verbalize it, the words won't even come
out? It leaves you with this icky,
sticky feeling inside, a feeling of
heavy hurt that doesn't
seem like it will ever go away. You're filled

with rage, with pain and horror,
yet nobody knows because it surpasses words.
It is beyond understanding, it would seem.
So you sit in silence, letting hot, choking tears
trickle down your face as you fight
for each breath and scrabble helplessly
for a solution that seems cruelly out of reach.

Captured Moments

Photos on the wall—
tracking the trajectory my life
has taken so far. Selfies at parties,
my siblings being strange, eating
with my roommates, my dogs' cute
little faces making me miss home.

These little glimpses of the past
can certainly be painful; some days,
the tears pierce my eyes if I stare
for too long. A lot of those people
I don't even talk to anymore. Who is left
that I can still call a friend?

But sometimes, it is nice to remember
the simpler times before all the pain
I've suffered in front of these photos,
crying in this tiny bedroom as life
overwhelmed me. I miss the moments
that they capture—ice cream at Walmart
in the dark, my brother dressed as an ear
of corn, delivering cookies in the cold,
parking lot carnivals, Target post-"prom,"

my cousin being a clown on many different
occasions. There is good up there too,
happy memories smiling upon my back
as I write this poem. And I know
there are more to come; it just doesn't feel
like it yet. I used to know how to have fun,
and I desperately hope I haven't lost that.

reality blurred

Sometimes I daydream myself into trouble,
to moments off the beaten path, each one crystal
clear yet simultaneously a blur,
where we drive aimlessly down the backroads,
take the longer route to spend more
time together, existing in our little bubble
of bliss. You are all I need, content just to drive
forever with you, so it feels so brutal
when these moments end. I want to tell you what
you mean to me, to blurt the words out,
but that isn't good enough. No amount
of words, not even a lengthy letter
would be the right way to explain myself, to tell
you what I miss about the little moments in my
mind and the happiness that they brought
to me. In those moments, we could adventure
and rebel, watching the airplanes soar overhead
and dreaming of the unlimited freedom of the
sky, blue against the black
of the road that defined
our own version of reality,
but then I snap out of it, remembering that that
isn't how things really are, the bubble bursting

a reminder that I'm alone, unlike our peaceful
drives, in a place terribly turbulent.

You Can Tell a Lot About a Girl by Her Collections

By her shoe closet…
Indecisive. She likes variety and having options
available. Lots of colors, lots of styles,
lots of fun!
She cares about how she looks. Clothes give her
confidence, and she wants to make
a good impression. She's complex,
and she definitely has personality.
Vans in six colors? Multiple pairs
of black ankle boots that could crush your toes
with a stomp? Any day's outfit
might present only one facet of her, but
whichever pair she wears, you can bet
they'll be well-kept and look brand new
and pair perfectly with her nerdy t-shirt
of choice.

By her record crate…
Maybe she's just here for the aesthetic.
If that's basic, then oh well. After all,
isn't that why record players came back
into fashion anyway?

Not that that matters; she just finds it
very comforting to lie down and let the records
spin while the music washes over her.
Sometimes, it's the simple pleasures
in life that get her through.
Her collection's not huge, but it showcases
some of her favorites. That seems like
a safe place to start
as a new collector, and from there,
it can always grow (it seems to expand rapidly
at Christmastime). And as she samples
more music (and saves her money),
she can afford to bravely explore
the further reaches of what the record stores
have to offer.

By her bookshelf...
More than you can count. A bookshelf so
crammed with beloved books
that it overflows, stack after stack waiting
for their pages to be turned or their spines to be
seated on shelves. (Nerd alert!) She's either
super smart or determined to escape reality,
or maybe both? I mean, with a mixture of
esteemed classics and young adult fantasy
(and some books that toe the line between the
two), it's very likely both. Her books' conditions
will vary – some were bought used, some

have been through her little brother's
ruthless backpack (which nothing escapes
unscathed), some are carefully tended
to remain in beautiful mint condition.
You might be able to guess
favorites by this, but then again, sometimes
the most worn down are the most well-loved.
And you shouldn't be surprised to find some
duplicates. She's a perfectionist
who likes her series in matching sets whenever
possible, and some copies are scribbled up
with annotations from high school English class,
something that won't go away any time soon –
the future English teacher's curse!
And if she's ever going to build a library to rival
Beauty and the Beast's in her future house,
she has to collect pretty volumes
worthy to line the shelves
and fill the space. Might as well start now!

the problem with poetry

My problem with poetry is that so much of it is written by those who have seen so much more of life than I. They write from a point of maturity that belongs to real adults, adults who have seen darkness and hardship and are just plain tired of it. So much of the worldview in the lens of their poems seems colored by cynicism and the "boringness" all children dread becoming. I don't know them, but I'm just being frank.

Perhaps it's inexperience talking, since here I stand, a poet of sorts myself. There is nothing in my hands but a pen and my desire to write about hope. I'm left pondering if my outlook on the world will be accepted by those of critical status. I am not a real adult; I am still just a teenager who could barely handle the mental strain of navigating an unfamiliar grocery store a few months ago. What wisdom do I have to offer the world? Is my ink wasted if I write of my joy? No, of course it isn't. The world needs it – now more than ever. But no matter how hard I try, I do not often write from a place of joy. Instead, my pen and my mind work in tandem to spill my pain and my politics as I fight to hold my tears inside. I am already becoming what I have feared.

I try to think happy thoughts, but Peter Pan would be disappointed in me in that regard. So much of my poetry stems from reality, not imagination; narration in verse feels forced to me, while venting my feelings simply flows. Thus I join the line of poets writing about their own lives, and I ask: do we still have faith that things can turn around? Do we still have laughter? And why can't we remain more like children in the ways that matter most?

I Refuse to Bow

The schools tried to change me.

They tried to mold me, to fold me
into the shape of a pretty little
liberal princess, a snow-
flaky young activist with no true
sense of the world.

They underestimated the strength of my
skeleton, of the ideals that hold my spine straight
and upright even under the pressure
of adversity. I will not be cowed.
I will not bow down. I do not listen
to what they say just because
they wield the power.
We the people can take it away. And I for one
am determined that we should do just that.

It's time for my generation to rise up.

fear.

Fear is a vampire,
a villain blocking your
path. He's a life ruiner,
a soul destroyer,
a killer who comes
for you in the darkness
to suck the life out
of you. Don't let him
walk through your door.
Do not invite him inside.
But if he's already there,
stake him right through
the heart and put an end
to his reign of terror.

Letters I'll Never Send

I've begun to write letters,
letters that I'll never send.

There they sit,
seething, angry,
leeching the rage out of my soul
and onto the page.

They're directed to people,
both near and far,
who have done something wrong.
They hurt someone, or many someones,
and I don't think they feel remorse for it.

I am angry at them,
but they will never even know.
Writing these words, if nothing else, brings
catharsis to my fuming soul.

I wish these people would apologize, really
apologize, and try to make amends.
But people are never that simple,
especially when they are cruel,
power-hungry ones.

I wonder if they'd learn to change
if only they knew what was written
in the letters that I'll never send.

Spaghetti Brain

Words are hard. They never want
to come out of my mouth right. Something
always ends up jumbled or goes missing
or gets lost in translation,
leaving a gap in understanding between
the two of us. I try so hard to stop
myself, to pause and think, but sometimes
the ideas pile up on one another
like cars colliding in a movie scene,
and I can't think straight because of the fear
of losing one in the ensuing chaos inside of me.
When I'm clutching at so many
slippery thoughts at once, it's easy to get
lost in my own brain,
and when I'm lost, I'm confused, which means
everyone is ultimately unsatisfied
with what I have to say.

Perhaps this is why I choose to write;
in this medium,
you can revise again and again
until the words feel just right
(though most of us will never be
totally satisfied with the result;

I'll look back at this poem in
the future and make silent
corrections to my own verse, like I always do).
Don't fault me for this frustration; it's the irony
of life as an English major.
And believe me, if your thoughts were
made of spaghetti,
your mind would be a little bit messy too.

warrior

She is a warrior.

You might not see it from the outside.
She doesn't march around in armor
or carry a sword or a bow strapped to her back.
Her arms are not loaded with strength,
and her skin does not bear the scars of battle.
She is not that kind of warrior.

"You always smile like you're about to cry."
She smiles through this too, all while thinking
Well, what else should I do?
Honesty shows vulnerability.
Trust lets people in.
And a smile is the toughest armor to crack.

my grief

My grief doesn't come with tears. It doesn't look
like it does on TV. I am not the *screaming,*
crying perfect storm that everyone expects
someone as emotional as me to be.
That isn't how it goes.
No, my grief comes with a heaviness that clings
to my soul, this weight of sorrow that hangs in
my mind, ever-present, unceasing. It constricts
my lungs, weighs me down until I can barely
breathe. I feel as if I have failed you,
and I wonder what would have happened
if the circumstances were different:
if I had been there when you died,
if I had listened just a bit more closely
when you spoke, if I had talked
to you just a little longer at birthday parties,
if I had tried to care about you as much
as I do about everybody else.
If we had had the kind of relationship between
grandparent and grandchild that I've heard
my friends talk about. But we didn't,
and I took you for granted as a fixture in my life.
I didn't realize when it would be the last
time we talked. I made a promise

to come back and see you each time, and I
couldn't do that. I don't know
that I'll ever stop being haunted by that,
so all I can say is
I'm sorry.

An Imaginary Elsewhere

In my mind, I am not here.
Left alone, I could be anywhere else,

a thousand other places
where I can take a breath
or focus on something significantly
more exciting than writing essays
and making grocery lists. I might be

fighting aliens as a superhero,
exploring hidden worlds through
secret passages in the woods,
navigating the chaos of reuniting
two kingdoms, meeting mythical
creatures, flying on the back
of a dragon, chasing monsters

to save someone else. In the realm
of my imagination, I can wield a sword,
shoot a bow with perfect aim, and keep
a tiara balanced on my head with no
effort. I dream of dancing until daybreak
at a magnificent ball or hunting down
a secret passage hidden inside

a library bookshelf or an antique
wardrobe. I read, I write, I watch

too many movies. In short, I'm
a daydreamer, cooking up an
imaginary elsewhere in my mind.
Pardon me if I seem a little bit distracted.

Celestine

She used to hate him.

Hated the arrogance that oozed from his smile,
hated the way he never listened
and the way he wouldn't let her finish
her sentences. He never seemed to care
what she had to say, and it showed.

They couldn't stand to be near
each other. The other's presence became
nearly intolerable, yet she could never
escape him.

Then the danger hit. And in the wild,
he proved his mettle. They fought
and they argued and they cried and they worried,
fear the only thing more potent than
the smell of the trees
and the anguish in their hearts.

She didn't expect to miss him when she fled,
but nevertheless, she felt something
was missing. She missed the sarcastic remarks

and matching smile of the sheltered boy
who thought he knew everything.
She couldn't fault him for it; she was
the same way, had been since birth. She missed
their animated debates and the swoop
of his hair and the glint in his eyes and the way
he teased her, the mischief that was always
at the forefront of his mind
and the affectionate way he talked
about his brother. She'd been wrong.
He really was kind, and she missed him.

She used to hate him, she really did.
She thought it would always stay that way.

But now she doesn't,
and that's good enough for a seed
of love to begin to blossom.

a poetic graveyard

We are gathered here today
to memorialize every poem that didn't
make the final cut – every poem that fell
too flat for class, sat sidelined from contests,
faced rejection from my blog, and even
watched its neighbors in Google Drive
be selected for this book while it was ignored.

I can't offer them much; I'm my own worst
critic, and as their writer, I fear
they may be too far gone for my help.
Some poems are simply a case
of "right idea, wrong time;" they may
see the light of day yet, if I can only
find the words to fill them.
Until then, R.I.P.:
rest in poetry.

soul sisters

You understand what I mean
when I cannot find the words
to finish a sentence. You laugh
at my jokes, and we can almost
speak a language that no one else
understands. Your wisdom is insightful,
your ideas are invaluable, your smile
is infectious. You roll up in my driveway
in your cute little Mini, and no matter
what we do, it will be an adventure.
Posing with fake fruit in Hobby Lobby,
confusing my family with our animated
conversations about movies or music
or celebrities, and losing our minds
on a spontaneous trip to Kings Island
and in the movie theater watching Spider-Man–
every moment with you, calm or chaotic,
can't help but make me smile. You listen,
you care, and together, we concoct dreams
of an incredible apartment, decorated
like it came off of Pinterest (but with a nerdy
touch). Any body-sized dents in the wall

from my clumsiness can be easily covered up
with life-sized cardboard cutouts
or some other funky prop, and we'll bake
so many cookies that we won't know
what to do with them. We'll spin our favorite
records and plot collaborative novels
and most of all praise the Lord
for His innumerable blessings, and we'll figure
out how to be adults without growing up.

an ode to Cinderella, in which the poet gets personal

She's everything you've already heard.
You'd be shocked to witness the transformation
from her everyday appearance to a look
that defines "dress to impress." Her shoe
collection is impeccable, awe-inspiring
even. She might seem quiet, meek,
overshadowed in many ways,
and she shelters in the comfort of her
animal friends. Her work never ends;
for each task completed, three more are
loaded on top of her existing workload,
yet she diligently presses on, doing the best
she can. Some nights she cries
herself to sleep, but mostly she dreams
of the future, another life, an escape. She dances
through her pain and takes comfort in the songs
she sings under her breath, too quiet
for anyone else to hear. She aims for
optimism and tries to see the best
in every situation, even if it takes
a sarcastic smile to get there.
She knows so little yet so much.

And to her, midnight matters.

Not because she will lose everything,
but because it is a pivotal point. A moment
of change. She must race against the clock,
fighting for every second she spends
waltzing around that ballroom. Is the risk
justified? What if nothing comes of it?
How will she recover from the hope
that shattered her heart, the closeness
of something so desired
yet utterly out of reach?

after midnight

After midnight is a time of creativity,
when the stars twinkle outside like sparks
of inspiration. Something in the darkness
and silence of the world, the peace
and inactivity of the surroundings
makes it perfect for my brain
to work. Combining dim lights
and closed windows with a lack
of obligation gives me an openness
not found in any other temporal
block. It is a time unclaimed
by work or school, cooking
or cleaning, meetings or homework,

and no one expects anything from me
because most other people aren't
awake. That little moment of beautiful
free time promises so much possibility…
if I can just stay awake that long.
Who needs sleep anyway?

the things they don't tell you

I used to believe adulthood was simple.
But now that I'm here, it most definitely
is not. The grocery store is overwhelming.
I get lost sometimes, and no one is going
to come over the store intercom and call
for me. I need money for food and self-restraint
not to spend it on an entire wardrobe or a full
shelf in my personal library. I have to
talk in uncomfortable conversations
about politics, which are a zillion times more
messy, ugly, and complicated than
my fifth-grade self would have dreamed
during our fake election. People are angry.
I am one of those people. The air
and the internet are rife with disagreement,
and what can I do to solve all the world's
problems? I miss my mom. This is too hard.
Friends told me from the TV, slowly
showing me how challenging adulting can be,
"Welcome to the real world! It sucks!
You're gonna love it." Roommates,
relationships, at times general idiocy…it
was all there from the moment
Rachel crashed in wearing a soaking

wet wedding dress. I want to get married
someday. I do still believe
in love. It would be a dream come true,
but even marriage isn't right in the movies. You
fight, you're confused, but yes, you should
still be happy. I want to be happy. What will
it take for me to be happy? I thought
this would be easier. I'm treading in deep water,
barely staying afloat, buoyed upward
only by prayer and hope
that my God knows what He is doing
when I don't.

www.ingramcontent.com/pod-product-compliance
Lightning Source LLC
LaVergne TN
LVHW051240200726

843510LV00011B/1632